JORDAN WIENKE

Start Your Mentorship Program

A Beginner Guide

PLATYPUS

PUBLISHING

To Mike Wienke, you know exactly why.

Contents

Foreword

There are a ton of books about mentoring programs. They tell you how to build a mentor program, how to be a mentor, or how to be a mentee. They talk about a mentor program's value to your company or organization. Their pages are filled with research and references. The authors are professional development people and take the time to explain each aspect and why.

They'll tell you mentoring programs:
  Improve personal and career development
  Improve on boarding
  Facilitate leadership development
  Build diversity
  Allies for reverse mentoring
  Support a learning culture
  Reduce costs

Maybe you've read them, and maybe you've tried them. Sadly, your efforts and good intentions have probably failed.

The flaw in those books isn't the research or the program, it's how people are paired, how they are brought into the program and the expectations. Without that human connection, setting of expectations and freedom to let the relationship organically grow true mentorship won't develop. You can make mentoring part of the job, you can require it, but forcing true connection never works. There needs to be intentional pairing or matching of people. Not necessarily based on job title or experience, but a deeper connection. Perhaps the people both like cycling, have the same undergraduate degree, read the same type of books. Giving something other than work, is the beginning.

Once paired, the training retreats and guidance you provide has to provide an opportunity to connect in those ways. A general discussion on similarities, the age old "get to know you" from summer camp followed by the reason for the mentor program – professional development. Creating those connections starts well before the pairs meet, and continues for the duration of the mentorship. My book takes you through this process of connecting people in a meaningful way so the actual work and benefit of a mentorship can occur.

I've run mentor programs, failed and succeeded. I want to share with you what I've learned and how to apply it to your organization now. This book will teach you to develop and launch a sustainable, meaningful mentoring program within your organization in one year. Yep. One. Year.

Before we go any further, I have to dispel a few key myths about mentorship programs.

1 - No, it will not take up your whole work week. You can accomplish everything in about an hour a week, sometimes much less.

2 - No, you will not have to answer a million questions about next steps. In fact, if you set things up correctly you should have very few follow up queries.

3 - No, I'm not going to give you pages of references or links. You will get step-by-step instructions with examples that are easy to follow.

4 - No, people won't think you're crazy for attempting yet another mentoring program. They'll think you're a genius.

If you're ready to take your organization to the next level quickly and efficiently. If you want to develop something unique for your employees or members, but are sure where to begin. If you've made it this far, then it's time to get started!

Acknowledgement

Thank you to Platypus Publishing for taking a chance on an idea. Thank you to my husband, Mike, who encourages me every day. Thank you to my daughter, Ryann, who self-created the cover art. Thank you to my son John for telling me not to worry so much. And thank you to my son James who tells me everything I write is "really good".

Chapter 1

Skip to Chapter 2 if you don't want to know who I am, and why this will work.

I've had a few jobs in my lifetime. I've worked in advertising, food and beverage, parks and recreation, and education (elementary and higher). For the most part I've been properly trained in my profession, on boarded with my colleagues, and overall prepared for the job I was hired for. Everything was technically sound.

But, I wanted something more. I wanted to connect and network, and frankly, networking wasn't "working" for me. I'd go to conferences or live stream seminars or online learning opportunities, they were good and helpful to learning, but not connecting me to someone else. I was outgoing and able to collect business cards with the best of them. I even connected on socials with some people, but I wasn't really *connecting*. When it came time to reach back out to one of my "connections", I had no idea where to begin this process. It felt forced and awkward to invent reasons to email someone, let alone call them on the phone. What was I supposed to say exactly? How would that conversation even go?

Then, as they say, an opportunity presented itself to me as a problem.

Before we get there, let's back up a bit. As I mentioned in the intro, I've launched a number of mentorship programs. My first attempt was when I was working in parks and recreation as an aquatic supervisor. Like many in my field, I didn't have enough lifeguards to keep my pool open. My staff was mostly part-time teenagers, so I spent big chunks of my time recruiting to replace staff that moved on to college or other parts of their lives. I needed a way to create a consistent stream of qualified candidates. I decided to start a Jr. Lifeguard mentoring program. Jr. Lifeguards would volunteer and be mentored by my regular lifeguards. If the Jr. Lifeguards volunteered for 30 hours, I'd train them to be fully certified lifeguards for free.

This program was a huge amount of work. I spent hours each week talking to Junior Lifeguards and Lifeguards and coordinating the pairing schedule. I set aside time to circle back around to make sure people were on the right track. I listened to my seasoned lifeguards as they gave me feedback on things that worked or didn't work. It was a pain, and hindered my ability to do my regular job of managing the whole aquatic center. Although it wasn't executed correctly, the concept behind the program was solid. CI learned to cultivate a pairing based on common interests outside of lifeguarding to ensure a cohesive pairing.

Fast forward a few years. I was volunteering as one of two

2

treasurers at my kids' elementary school on the Parent Teacher Organization (PTO). We had very little overlap with the outgoing treasurer, so we were thrust into the position with little training and left to figure things out. I realized swiftly that no transition plan existed and I was determined to leave the next generation of volunteers with a better strategy than "Here is the notebook and software, ask questions if you need to and have fun!" Immediately, I suggested developing a transition plan. I created a manual with directions, a timeline and accountability forms. What started as an outline for the next iteration of treasurers quickly grew into a general manual for the PTO at large. I talked to the other members to get a sense of their roles and responsibilities to add to the living document. By outlining job descriptions and transition plans for every position each generation would have a place to start, and a pathway forward.

I brought all of this to the PTO and we were able to look at those who were interested in coming onto the PTO, brainstorm who would work best with whom and why. The thought was this would make the mentoring process more personalized. Once we landed on the pairs, we asked those on the shortlist to be mentored and brought up in the PTO. And..it worked! At the end of our two year term we had successfully executed the transition, new people were trained and in place. Everyone felt good about the transition. And it was smooth sailing.

I'd like to sit here and brag to you that it's been smooth sailing ever since. That would be a lie.

It was not sustainable. Those who took over tried their best, but life happened. Things got in the way, and leaders left. Transition died. Aside from the google docs and remnants of the beloved manual, all that work was gone.

Now to the place where the problem as opportunity occurred.

Continuing further along on my path. I was at a conference for NACADA (National Academic Advising Association). I joined one of the many communities and volunteered for the graduate and professional student advising steering committee. During a meeting, someone asked the question, "How do we bring other professionals up and into this niche advising field?" I raised my hand and said, "We should do a mentor program." I should have known that's how you end up running the thing you suggested, which is exactly what happened.

I asked for help getting things going in the right direction, and three people joined me. We researched and reviewed other mentor programs that had successes in the past. We met and brainstormed. I took notes, developed a timeline and processes. Connected with the right people to get advertising out about our program and promote it. Then I sat down and wrote the manual and built the program from our meetings in just a few short months.

From my past experience in the Jr. Lifeguarding mentor program I knew we needed to be intentional about pairing people. From my experience on the PTO I also knew this program needed a way to be sustainable. Finally, I needed to make sure that our initial sub committee had a solid exit strategy to slowly move on to other opportunities.

Over the next two years I used feedback to continually shape the handbook. I developed a transition plan, accepted applications, created monthly check-in newsletters, collaborated to create entry and exit surveys to measure success, communicated with participants and launched a successful mentor program. Our committee worked together well, and the response was overwhelmingly positive. It was more successful than I could have imagined. We have turned over committee members and I too, am transitioning on, confident that the program will move forward into the future successfully. In 2022, I was nominated and won the ACD Service Award from NACADA for my work with the mentoring program, which inspired me to put the process down on paper and share it with the world.

Today I can say that if you feel like you've been missing out, if you feel like you want something more for yourself or for your employees, company or organization, I can teach you how to establish and launch a sustainable mentoring program in one year.

Chapter 2

Roll up your sleeves. Let's do this!

Establish a committee.

You'll need one **point person** to set the mentoring program up for success. Continuity is essential in the early stages, so this person must be able to commit to at least two full years as the point person during the initial setup, although three is ideal. It's important to note that only the initial point person will commit to two years; in the future, the point person will only need to commit to one year.

This point person will arrange meetings, send zoom links, be the secretary, send out reminders, set agendas, and do all the grunt work. They need to be someone who understands how to run an efficient meeting. Someone who understands that time is valuable, agendas should be short, and emails should provide information well in advance. Organization and efficiency should be words others use to describe them, as well as words they use to describe themselves. Again, this is a two-year commitment - one year of establishing/coordinating and one year of shadowing and helping transition the next point person.

As the point person, you'll be the driving force behind the mentor program, but you'll also need two or three committed team members. It's important for these people to have a vested interest in participating in this endeavor. Voluentolding people won't work. The committee members need only be interested in one thing, getting this program going.

Now that you have your 3 - 4 person committee, it's time to establish who will be **the successor** - the person who take the reins after the point person has finished their two-year commitment. In the first year, the successor is there to observe and understand. This gives them time to learn and develop the solid formation needed to take over the following year and subsequently have a successor shadowing them the year they are the point person. And so on each year afterward someone shadows and the following year someone takes over.

Lifespan Of A Mentor Point Person				
Year One	Year Two	Year Three	Year Four	Year Five
PP1	PP1	PP2	PP3	PP4
CM	PP2s	PP3s	PP4s	PP5s
CM	CM	CM	CM	CM
CM	(CM)	(CM)	(CM)	(CM)
	CM	PP1	PP2	PP3

PP = Point Person

CM = Committee Member

s = shadow

Shaded is the year they are no longer on the committee

Shaded is the year they are no longer on the committee, unless they want to.

For the other committee members, their commitment is for one year, unless they choose to stay around for another. No more than four people should ever be on the committee. More than that and things get bogged down, the ability to run a quick efficient meeting is diminished. Four is the ideal number for efficiency. Ideally, you'll have four members to get things off the ground in the first year. After that it's possible to manage with just three.

Setting up these roles each year before you start your timeline for the year is critical to success. When everyone knows their role and responsibility on the committee, it's easier for them to understand what they are being asked to do and commit the time required for the program to be a success. The trick to getting people to commit and sustain a mentoring program is letting those running the program to know up front what the commitment is and when they can step down with the knowledge that all the work they've done won't be for nothing. Sometimes it helps to write "job descriptions" that include weekly time commitments, so that those who volunteer know exactly what they are getting into. And that is really what you want, commitment to a sustainable program for years to come.

SAMPLE Job Descriptions

Point Person

Responsible for arranging meetings, sending zoom links and invites, being the secretary for all meetings, emailing reminders, setting agendas, keeping to the timeline, answering any questions about the program and sending all correspondence to all mentors and mentees and managing two yearly group meetings. Training the next point person. Needs to be highly skilled in time management and meeting organization.

Time Commitment

Approximately 17 hours a year, broken down below.
Jan – March: 1 hour per month
April: 2 hours

May: 3 hours
June: 3 hours
July: 2 hours
August – October: 1 hour per month
November – December: total about 1 hour

Committee Member

Responsible for coming prepared for and actively attending meetings, keeping to the timeline, running two yearly group meetings. Emailing out monthly newsletter. Must be committed to coming prepared to every meeting initiated by the point person.

Time Commitment

Approximately 15 hours a year, broken down below.
Jan – March: about 2 hours total
April: 2 hours
May: 3 hours
June: 3 hours
July: 2 hours
August – October: about 2 hours total
November – December: about 1 hour total

Chapter 3

Meetings.

No meeting should ever go more than one hour. Most will be shorter. The point person needs to make that clear at the first meeting and hold the committee to that plan. It's important to know that you'll have more meetings during the first year, as you're setting the foundation of the program. This is because the group will need to dive deep into laying the foundation for the program guidelines. In the following years, the number of meetings will decrease.

Meeting Rules

- *Agenda and all relevant items for review will be sent out two full working weeks prior to the meeting:* Meaning, applications, sample questions, research to be read, etc. everything. When sending the agenda with attachments to be reviewed remind everyone they have to come prepared to discuss
- *No "additional items" will be added after agenda is set:* Anything that needs adding after the agenda will be added to the next meeting

- *Everyone gets to talk:* You have four members and you're one of them, so everyone gets a say, take good notes
- *Move onto the next item on agenda:* Do not linger or circle back around
- *Start on time, finish on time:* If you run out of time, add it to the next meeting to continue discussion
- *Send out summary and completed "rough drafts" for review if necessary for added input:* Do not waste time in a meeting hashing out opinions, that can easily be taken into consideration in an email

Meeting 1

Establish your point person, successor and committee members.

Develop rules and regulations for your mentor program.
You'll need to decide:
Start date and duration
Application deadlines
Define mentor / mentee
Who can apply
Length of commitment
Modality of program
Questions on application

Start Date and Duration

I recommend that no mentor program last more than one year. That doesn't mean the people won't connect for years to come, just that the formal commitment ends after one year. Finding an event to tie to your program works well. I recommend a large convention, annual meeting or fiscal year at the beginning and end of your program. Using a fixed and standard starting and ending point for the mentor program allows participants to know exactly when their time in the program begins and ends. It also makes it easy for people to remember.

Application Deadlines

Application deadlines should be established after you determine when your program will begin and end. About 2-3 months is a good window to accept applications, but you can make the window shorter or longer as you see fit. Applications should NOT take hours to complete, but should ask good solid questions about the person and their experience so that you can quickly learn who they are as a whole person and who would be best to match them with.

Role Definitions

Defining the role of mentor and mentee means clarifying category parameters. For example, when we set up our NACADA program we determined that a mentee should be someone with less than one year in advising, mentors then needed more than one year. We did argue this point a bit as some people have other experience that could be counted as academic advising. But we decided that for the parameters of our program, we would publish it that way. We verbally left the door open for some flexibility there, as we knew there were people who had other experiences that could be counted. But we had to pick something to go with, so we picked the one-year mark.

Who Can Apply

This is important because getting the right mix of people

can make or break a program. If you *require* people to do this, they are not invested. If you are a professional organization, you might want to consider how long they have been a member. A professional business, length of time in the profession. Whatever you pick, remember, you want them invested but not excluded, it's a fine line. You really want people who are invested in committing to one full year of mentorship. If that happens to be someone who only recently joined your organization or group but has experience elsewhere you may not want to rule them out. Don't make the mistake of making this too restrictive, or no one will be interested. On the flip side, don't make it so easy that everyone can do it.

Length of Commitment

Organized mentorship should not last more than one calendar year. More than that and people feel trapped, or that they don't have the time to invest. Less than that and a relationship is unlikely to develop. One year, that doesn't seem so bad, and if you break it up correctly, it will fly by. Again, the connection may last longer, but the commitment is minimal.

During this part of the discussion you'll need to decide on what you will require of your participants. This is a delicate balance between too many touch points and not enough. If you're unsure I recommend a once a month check in at a minimum. Pairs or small groups of no more than three, will meet once a month for one hour. More time can be added, but this is the selling point for the program. A professional or volunteer asked to give 12 - 15 hours a year sounds minimal. Again, the pairs or groups may meet more, but that is the minimum commitment.

Modality of Program

The modality of the program should also be reviewed. The world has changed in wonderful ways live virtual meetings (Zoom, WebEx, Teams, Google Meet, etc.) is one of those ways. I recommend live virtual meetings, this enables people from all over the world to be able to participate. People work from home more often now, work places are flexible, your mentor program should be flexible as well. Obviously you are welcome to require this be all in person, but I believe you'll lose good people that way. However, if your organization, group or company all work close to each other, and are comfortable coming together in person regularly you can also easily do this in person.

Application Questions

Questions on the application can lead to a long meeting and a long discussion. I recommend emailing the committee and asking each member to contribute 2-3 questions for the application about one week before the first initial meeting. Have them email the point person individually, not to the group. You will likely see overlap, which shows your group is on the same page, and will highlight good questions. You can then compile these into *one page only*, more than that and it will feel overwhelming. Email it to the group along with the agenda a week before the meeting for everyone to review. This way when you come to the discussion point regarding application, you're not starting from scratch and having a long meeting.

As you build your application, think about the experience of the application. Don't make the applications so long that it will take the applicant a full workday to complete. But, make the questions long enough to force the applicant to think for a minute before answering. Sample questions are included at the end of this book.

Finally, while not necessary, I recommend you put a few mandatory requirements on the application. For example:

Applying means you are committing to a one-hour meeting every month, that you will read the monthly newsletter, attend the initial launch training and attend virtually two touch base sessions during the year.

Or

Applying means you are committing to this one-year mentorship program.

It's not necessary to put everything on the application, but you want those who do apply to understand up front what they are committing to. You're trying to craft an application so that those who apply 1) know what they are getting into 2) are committed to doing this for one full year.

Once that is set, the point person will take everything and start creating the rough draft of the manual as well as the timeline and marketing materials.

Meeting 2

Prior to the second meeting during the first year only, the point person will need to build the handbook from the information gathered in the first meeting. This is not as scary as it seems since you already had the first meeting with the group to develop all elements of this handbook. The point person will also establish a timeline built backward from the start/end point of the year-long mentorship program. Both the timeline and the rough draft of the mentor handbook will need to be emailed two weeks prior to the next meeting.

Between the first meeting and the second meeting the point person will need about 5-10 hours of time to create the handbook and the timeline. That IS a lot of time. If you took good notes in the first meeting, it should be as simple as organizing the notes into a cohesive document. You're not inventing anything new, you're organizing the group's thoughts and decisions from the first meeting. Renaming the headings and flushing out the notes. The better you are at taking notes, the faster this process will go. Remember, this is your first year. The first year is the hardest on the point person, after your program is set up and running the time commitment for the point person will be significantly reduced. Keep in mind while organizing all this information that this is not set in stone, this is a living breathing document that is used to shape your mentor program and each iteration afterward will change slightly based on feedback from participants and committee members. Don't put pressure on yourself to "get it right" the first time, that is NOT what this handbook and timeline are about.

Agenda points for your second meeting should include:
   Review of the handbook
   Final review of application questions
   Review of timeline
   Discussion on how/where to market or publicize the program

Discussion on when to review applications

The group should have already gotten a copy of the application, handbook and timeline. Any conversation on this can happen now. Keep an open mind while discussing and remember, this *needs to be a living document.* Things change, these things are not hard and fast. Your program needs to live on beyond year one, two etc..

Marketing or publicizing is very important and brainstorming is a great way to approach this. How are you going to do this? Who will do this? This is important to establish. You may have regional meetings where you could send a press release, memo, or email. What about internal or external newsletters? Look at the timings of these meetings. You don't want to overwhelm people, and you also want to ensure that your program's marketing fits with the application deadlines. You don't want to send out teasers in December if your deadline is May 1st. Talking through where you can promote with the group is always good. Social platforms, professional or otherwise, can also be a good channel if appropriate to your target group. Your group will know best. Chapter 4 goes into more detail on how to market.

Ultimately the point person will take all this information and develop a marketing timeline that coincides with the application deadlines. Complete with contact emails so that next year you can rinse and repeat. You can also adjust over the years, adding or subtracting contacts based on input from your program and others.

Remember, you determine to send out or disseminate the applications you've developed, the point person needs to not only collect applications, but be available to answer questions via email or phone should they arise. You may think this will take a lot of time, but, questions should be minimal if you've designed the application and marketed it correctly. I suggest the point person start an email folder or drive-based folder to hold all the applications, make sure to put the date in the label so that you know which mentor year you are looking at.

Lastly, you'll need to decide when you'll meet to discuss applications. I recommend that after your application deadline the point person waits one week, for stragglers, then emails all applications to all committee members for review. Provide two to three weeks for review, and then ask people to put together their recommendations for pairs or small groups of three. Because the next time you meet, you'll be establishing pairs or small groups.

Meeting 3

Before this third meeting, where applications will be reviewed, the point person should send an email or follow-up to all applicants confirming their desire to be in the program and confirming their commitment of one full year to the program. Occasionally you may get a response from an applicant who is changing jobs, or moving, and those applications should be removed from consideration. This is also a good time to refresh the memory of those who applied of what the required dates of any touch point meetings, training, or other mandatory requirements are. This is not an email about acceptance to the program, just a "Hey, you applied. Do you still have the time and want to do this?" email. Give about a week or a specific date to respond. Remember, life happens. People change jobs, get puppies, and buy houses. You want to confirm that they are in this for the year. Once you have confirmation from all applicants, you can begin planning for your committee meeting.

The only thing on this agenda is setting up pairs or groups of three. While there is only one agenda topic, this can take the full hour. The point person should send all the application materials to the committee at least three weeks before this meeting. Each committee member should plan to review all the applications and do their own pairing or grouping of people before the meeting begins. Not all these pairs will match, and that's ok, it's important for the committee to review them individually.

At this meeting each person will explain whom they paired and why. Sometimes you'll see that others felt the same or similar. If that happens it's highly likely you have a good match. The point person should be keeping track of these pairs.

During this meeting you will also address any odd number issues. Pairing is the best way, but when that won't mathematically work, here are some of the ways I've worked around this.

Identifying a mentee who perhaps has experience to become a mentor. Occasionally I have had people with plenty of experience who are a bit shy, or need some more information. They have made excellent mentors. Asking a very experienced mentor to take on two mentees. Not ideal, but can work in a pinch with someone who is open to the idea of taking on two mentees. As applications come in and BEFORE the application deadline, if you notice the numbers are starting to stack up more heavily on the mentor or mentee side, ask the committee if they have anyone who they think would be a good candidate who has yet to apply.

Above all, resist the temptation to have committee members be mentors, this will mean more time commitment, create burnout, and frankly will make others not want to join the committee in the future. The committee is here to organize and work to make sure the mentors and mentees have a positive experience, NOT to be mentors themselves.

When dividing the people into pairs or groups, consider the length of time they've been in their role as well as the field. Sometimes the best mentors have only been in the field for a short time, but have vast experience that is translatable. These people sometimes want to be in the program as a mentee, not a mentor, which is completely understandable, these are things that will need to be discussed if they come up in this meeting. I have called people on several occasions and simply asked, "Why did you pick applying to be a mentee over a mentor?" That opened up the conversation and if you listen to their rationale you'll understand better what they want from the program and if they would be a better fit as a mentor.

Once the groups are decided upon, it will be up to the point person to reach out to the groups. Connect each pair via email, congratulate them, and list the:

- General welcome to the program
- Start and end date of mentorship
- Meeting and training requirement dates and times

An example of this email is listed at the back of this book.

Once all communication is out to the pairs, you can begin planning the first retreat.

Chapter 5 covers retreats and gives you a sense of what you might want to put in your power point.

Chapter 4

Marketing.

If you want this program to be a success, you're going to have to tell people about it. The committee will need to decide whether to market it big or small in the first year. Start by looking at what communication is already going out to people in the field. Consider listservs that go out through a regional, state, national or global professional organization, and collect those organizations' contact information. Internal and external monthly newsletters are also good. Think of all the communications received about your profession on a daily, monthly, or annual basis. Make a list. What are the socials? Are there LinkedIn, Facebook, or Twitter accounts that are controlled by those organizations? Collect all contact information. Once you have a solid list with contact information, begin crafting the communication.

Remember, each type of marketing must be tailored to the specific type of channel. Tweets are limited in the number of characters that can be used. More than a short paragraph on Facebook or LinkedIn and people lose interest. Email can be lengthier, however, people are busy, you want the who, what, when, where, why to be flashy and attention grabbing in the first two sentences. This is not something that needs to be covered in the committee, but something created by the point person. Once communications have been developed, send them to the committee for review. Then place the communication on the timeline.

Social media needs to be planned last, as this is the most quickly moving. Do not post your mentor program on social media three months before the applications are due, it will be confusing to those who use socials, and it will be forgotten. This should be shared a week or two before the applications are due. Monthly newsletters need to be planned out accordingly, make sure you place content in the newsletters one month before the application is due. Regional or state meetings and conferences can have a bit more substance, perhaps a flyer or even an email communication depending on what your contact is willing to do.

Be sure to set everything up and put the launch in your calendar as part of this process. At each touch point along the way, the point person sends out this messaging. Again, once the initial marketing communication is written, there should only be tweaking each year afterward.

All marking communication should include:

- Application deadline
- One year commitment
- 2 or 3 important dates

If you stick to this simple messaging, it's more likely you will attract applicants that are interested and devoted to your program. The more information you can provide to them in the initial marketing the better.

Newsletters

The next part of the marketing that you'll need to set up will be the monthly newsletter for your program. This is the point in time to essentially write all 10 months of communication. An outline is good, and you can leave a section free to place relevant information or poignant article. You can get creative about this and name it something snappy, "Mentor Monthly Minute" or more professional, "Mentor Newsletter", but the content should follow a consistent format.

Since your participants will be working in pairs or groups of three, the first part of the newsletter should highlight a member of the mentor group. Collect fun information from all accepted mentor participants. You can ask questions like, "What got you interested in this field?" or "Words of advice for those who want to advance their careers." Two or three get-to-know you questions are perfect. You don't want the entire newsletter to be about one person, but a few are good and allow the group as a whole to get to know each other a bit better each month.

The next section of the newsletter should give the pairs something to discuss or think about. This can be anything from an interesting article, or a nugget on how to work with your mentor/mentee. You can provide a question for the pair to discuss, to help get a conversation started - anything to keep that fire going for them. Sometimes even the best match can get stuck, and this next section should help get them over any hump. Some pairs will not need this nudge, others will grow from it.

Lastly you can end on a quote, or a link or a reminder of the next group touch point. If there is a yearly conference, adding that information can also be helpful. Sometimes there won't even be a next section of the newsletter. These newsletters are meant to inspire and introduce, not to go on for pages and get pushed to the bottom of the pile. Examples are included at the back of this book.

While designing the newsletter, remember, not all groups will need it. Some of them will leave your initial training with a plan already in place. Keep these newsletters short and simple. These are guides only, and help the group succeed as needed.

Chapter 5

Retreats.

Really, you can call this anything you want. A retreat, a training, an introduction. The name is irrelevant. The content is critical.

This initial retreat should include:

- Defining mentor/mentee
- Quotes
- Introductions
- Exercises to set goals
- Meeting times

Each of these are important to cover. The initial retreat should take about 2 hours and will likely be the longest one they are required to attend. This meeting should be mandatory as the pairs will work closely together to set up a plan of action for the next year and get to know each other.

Each of the 3 or 4 committee members, should have a role. You'll have to meet and do a dry run through of this initial retreat. The point person will develop the 2-hour presentation but each member should have equal responsibilities. If you review the example you'll see that much of this two-hour retreat is having the pairs work together in breakout rooms. This is intentional. This meeting will set the tone for the whole year for them, they need this time. Take your time with this, take the entire 2 hours if needed, it's important.

This is designed to be synchronous, or in person, the modality is irrelevant.

The first part should be introductions to the committee members who set up this program. General information about who they are, not a full resume, but you want those participating to know who the people are that are running this show.

Next, quotes about mentoring from something you've read or past mentor groups. You can also show a video of something fun or quirky about mentoring, maybe a Peanuts cartoon, nothing offensive, but something light. Just a little fun to start the retreat off. This isn't necessary but helps set the tone for the retreat.

Introductions of the group are next. For groups of 20 or more, it's ok to skip this part. You don't want to waste 20 minutes having each person talk for a minute or two. Instead, have them introduce themselves in a chat box for synchronous or you can do a roll call in person, just name and title and mentor/mentee. Again, this should be quick.

The first real exercise for this retreat will be having the pairs meet with each other. Give them about 5 minutes to list things they have in common that are not necessarily work related. Finding common ground beyond the reason you're there can help begin to forge a more personal relationship for the pairings moving forward.

Then bring the group back together for some discussion on what mentoring is and how it's defined. You can find third-party definitions, or you can work as a group to define this. Either way, it's important to make sure that this is where you explain the relationship goes both ways and requires commitment from both parties. At this point they should already know this, as they have applied and are willing to work toward this together. You can also talk about the importance of being willing and open to share, grow and learn through this process. Remind them that learning and growing goes both ways and is important to the process.

The group needs to also collectively reflect on previous mentor experiences. Sharing with the group, if they wish. Have them think of someone who previously mentored them, either officially or unofficially. What was good or bad about that experience? What did they learn? What did they gain? If you are in person, be sure to write this down on a large board, if online, just have the group talk about it.

Included next, you'll need to touch on the benefits to the mentor as well as the mentee. Why this is important for both parties and how it is important. While some may know all of this, it's always a good idea to refresh memories and bring it to the forefront during this time.

Remember to plan breaks as people (even synchronous people) need to stand, stretch, get water, head to the bathroom. This is a good stopping point before diving into the next part.

After the break you'll want to break them into two groups, all the mentees together and all the mentors together. These groups will make a list of their expectations for this program. It also gives them a chance to talk to one another separately from their pairs. This is also an opportunity for them to hear what others are thinking about this process and perhaps get ideas. Take about 5-10 minutes for this part, depending on group size.

When you bring everyone back, you'll have an open discussion, allowing each group the floor to discuss what their expectations are. One group will go then the other, order does not matter.

This is always a lot for the group, so the next part can be general expectations for the program. You can use this moment to remind the group collectively of monthly e-newsletter, or social platforms, conferences coming up or the next official meeting for the full group.

Preparing for the partnership needs to be covered next. You can find TED talks and other videos that discuss this. The video should cover what both mentor and mentee should do to prepare for the upcoming year. What each should be preparing to bring. I recommend you use a video as it breaks up the speaker responsibilities. Something that speaks to your constituents and is fresh and relevant works best.

Goals are a good way to help the pairs set expectations. I

use SMART Goal setting (Zachary & Fischler, 2012), but if you have something else that works, feel free. I've included the worksheet at the end of this book for your reference. I do not recommend that goals be set at this retreat. Goals should be set and determined by the groups at their first meeting. This will get them going in the right direction, and give them a topic for their first meeting.

Now the pairs are ready to be put back together again, this time they will set up their calendars with meeting dates. The expectation is that the pair will meet once a month, at a minimum. They are welcome to meet more, but that is the expectation. Have them break out to set up calendars. I recommend about 5-7 minutes for this.

Finally, as you bring the group back together I like to end by having them think about how they want to remember this experience in a year. What does that look like for everyone? How can they contribute so that they can ensure the outcome? This can sometimes help re frame things, so they internally reflect how they are going to guarantee success this year.

And that ends the first retreat.

The second retreat should be at the halfway mark. This one should be no longer than an hour. During this retreat each pair will share out where they are, what projects they are working on and how things are going in general. I like to make this one light-hearted. Silly hats, fun zoom background, or a fun quick game are also a good idea. This is also the place to snap a picture of the group.

Chapter 6

Surveys

You'll need to do bench marking, surveys are the best way to do this. I use Qualtrics, but you can use any methodology that is easy and convenient for you.

The point person should put this together with input from the committee. It should be tweaked each year to ensure that everything is correct and relevant to what the program is trying to achieve.

Here are some questions you may want to consider:

Initial Survey

What do you hope to gain from joining this program?

Mentorship is a partnership; we learn from each other. Please name two or three things that you hope to learn from your mentor/mentee.

What are the most important qualities of an effective mentor/-

mentee?

I know where to go to find resources in my field.

I know professionals and counterparts at other organizations whom I can reach out to for support.

I have the knowledge to confidently be a part of this organization or company.

Exit Survey

What did you hope to gain from joining the mentor program?

Did the Mentor Program meet your expectations? In what ways, please elaborate.

Mentorship is a partnership, we learn from each other: What did you learn from your mentor/mentee?

Do you feel you have new resources to assist you in your future endeavors?

Have you met new professionals and counterparts at other organizations or departments who you can reach out to for support?

Other questions to consider would be about value, overall satisfaction, experience, would you participate again, would you recommend, and additional comments. I always like additional comments as an opportunity to get new ideas if someone is willing to share.

Chapter 7

Where to go next year, and the next year and the next.

The beginning of this book I said the first year would be the hardest as setting it up is necessary. However, once established with the point person, successor and one or two other committee members moving into subsequent years is a snap.

At the end of each year, be sure to hold a meeting to review the surveys and ask if anything needs to change. Keep an open mindset. Remember, this is fluid, and needs to be adjusted based on changing landscape or the company or organization and new information that may come along. Use any helpful feedback from the surveys to guide changes you want to make. Freshen up the quotes for the initial retreat. Did someone find a video that might work better than the one used last year? Bring ideas to the table, that are helpful. Set up the new timeline for the upcoming year. This is also the time to have the successor officially take the helm as the point person. A new committee member will take over the monthly newsletter and will move into the successor position. If new members are needed due to turnover, you can introduce them into the process. Use this as a time to set up next year moving forward.

Some years nothing needs to change, some years you may need to re-think your newsletter or elements of your retreat. The last thing you want to do is keep things stale. Always refresh something a little. Keep it moving forward, in that way no one will get attached and fall into a rut with the program. Which will in turn keep the program feeling relevant and alive.

Chapter 8

Recognition

If there is an annual meeting or conference be sure to get some screen time/stage time or whatever you can get to publicly acknowledge those who dedicated a full year to this mentorship. You can also use socials, just to get the word out and congratulate the group, both mentors and mentees.

I also think there is merit in creating a certificate of completion. This is a relatively small expense and can go a long way in recognizing those who participated. When possible, have the committee sign the certificates before sending them, it gives it a more authentic feel. If not possible, still send certificates of completion. Something for the resume.

Chapter 9

Bumps

Yes, there will be bumps, I know this. Here are a few I've encountered and how I solved them:

What to do if I have more mentors than mentees or vice versa?
Review the applications, see if there are mentors who could be mentees, or mentees who could be mentors. You can also look at a group of three, if the dynamic works. I do not recommend going with more than three in a group.

I don't want to be a mentor/mentee, I want what I applied for.
You can do a few things with this. You can choose to honor the original request, and move on to the next person. You can offer them the spot of their choice for next year, giving them two years, one on each side of the fence. Or you could offer personal guidance through the first month or two. That one is time-consuming, but if you are willing to, it can be a good solution.

I'm leaving the field, but still want to participate.
You need to ask a few more questions here. Will you be

returning to the field? Are you going into a different field? Does the person simply not want to participate any longer?

My mentor/mentee is not responding.

Much of this would have been addressed when you reconnected to make sure everyone was on board for a year, but this can happen anyway. I found connecting on socials is a quick way to resolve this, just ping the person and ask if they are still interested in the program. You can also call the person. Unfortunately, if you cannot reach the person, then they are out, and you can add the person to another pair, or ask the person what they want to do.

APPENDIX

APPENDIX

<u>1</u>

General Timeline

January - February: Develop and refine handbook with committee members

February – March: Promote and market application and program

March - Half-way workshop

April: Application deadline for mentors/mentees

May - June: Review applications with committee and create pairs

July: Announce mentor/mentee pairs and send welcome emails with invitation to

workshop

August - September: Virtual workshop and evaluations (entry/exit)

September: Yearly start and end point of program AND recognition of previous year

participants

October – June: Monthly newsletters to mentor/mentees
November – December : Review materials for next year

2

Mentor Program Handbook
Purpose:
Why are you doing this?
What are the benefits?
What is the commitment?

General Requirements for Mentee:
Keep this simple, and easy. Membership in an organization?
Time in a position or at the company?
Add the commitment here as well: one year, meeting once a month, etc.

General Requirements for Mentor:
Same as for Mentee.

Benefits:
Mentor
List here.
Mentee
List here.

3

SMART Goals (Zachary & Fischler, 2012)

Specific: Be sure your goal is as specific as possible.

Example: I would like to be promoted to Management in the next two years.

Measurable: What are small check-ins you can do with yourself to make sure you are accomplishing your goal?

Example: I will develop a timeline for my year, breaking it down by month. It will include

meetings to attend and projects to work on that will give me exposure to management

position responsibilities.

Attainable: What resources do you need to accomplish your goal?

Example: My Mentor will connect me to people and invite me to any appropriate meetings.

Reasonable: What sacrifices do you need to make in order to accomplish your goal?

Example: I will dedicate 1 - 2 hours per week working on projects outside of my normal

work duties for the management exposure.

Timely: What is your final deadline?

Example: I would like to be promoted two years from the start of this program.

4

Action Plan Worksheet

Name:_____ Date:_____

Expectations for my mentoring partnership:_____

Partnership Goal

1:_____ 2: _____ 3:_____

Partnership Goal

1:_____ 2: _____ 3:_____

5

MARKETING

SOCIALS

The Mentor Program supported by <your organization> is pleased to announce that applications are open for the one-year Mentor Program which will specialize with this specific population.

Mentor and Mentee applications are now open and due <day/-date/year>. Details can be found <insert your web-link> on the <organization Web-Site>.

— —

<Company or program name> has launched a new Mentoring program. We are currently accepting applications for both mentors and mentees to apply. Applications are due <day/date/year>

Details can be found <insert your web-link> on the <Web-Site>.

EMAIL

Drum roll please.........<name of your program or company> Mentor Program

IS HERE!

The inaugural <name of program> Mentor Program supported by <company name> are pleased to announce a one-year Mentor Program which will specialize with this specific population.

Mentor and Mentee applications and details coming in <month/year>.

CONFERENCE ANNOUNCEMENT

<Company Name> just launched a <name of> Mentoring program. We are asking regions to post to their social media, and/or conference apps such as Whova if appropriate to promote this new mentoring opportunity.

Details can be found on the <insert web-site>.

6

Mentee Application
Must have less than 2 years with this specific population

Please submit applications directly to: <insert email address here>
   Your name, company, contact information
   Number of years in field and relevant work
   Number of years in other fields and relevant work

Are you currently a member of a professional organization or management team?

Additional background:

How did you get into your field?

What did you study in college?

Do you hold a master's degree or PhD? If so– in what?

Things you like to do in your free time.

Why do you want to be a part of this program?

Anything else you would want to include?

7
Mentor Application

Please submit applications directly to: <insert email address>

Your name, company, contact information

Number of years in field and relevant work

Number of years in other fields and relevant work

Are you currently a member of a professional organization or management team?

How did you get into your field? What is your story?

Additional background:

How did you get into your field?

What did you study in college?

Do you hold a master's degree or PhD? If so– in what?

Things you like to do in your free time.

Why do you want to be a part of this program?

Do you have any specialties?   Training and development? Writing and publishing?

Presenting at conferences?

Anything else you would want to include?

8

Mentor Program Check-In Monthly Email Newsletter Example:

Happy October!

Welcome to the Mentor Program monthly newsletter. We are hoping that you and your partner had time during the initial mentor meeting to set up your monthly meeting. While your meetings can be about best practices, information sharing or giving advice, we are also providing a few things to ponder as you move through this program.

Introductions:

In this section we will highlight people in the program so you can get to know

everyone in the group.

This month I'd like to introduce you to:

Name/Title

What is your biggest work accomplishment to date?

How did you come to this field?

What is a recent challenge you faced and what was your solution?

Any words of wisdom or advice?

ORGANIZATION:

We'll put information about <organization> in this space for you to enjoy.

Annual Conference, <day/date/year>

Regional Conferences a great way to connect

ONE DEVELOPMENT TOPIC PER MONTH EXAMPLES

Development Topic

Here is where you can find your "topic" for the month. While other items can certainly be discussed, this is a great way to narrow your focus throughout this program. This month focuses on your goals for this program. What can you work on this month? What are the challenges? Do you have a project you'd like to accomplish over the course of the year? Perhaps apply to present at a conference (state, regional, or national), create your working philosophy? What is one weakness that you want to make into a strength this fall?

* * *

Development Topic:

What was your career journey? How have you traversed higher education and advising within this industry? How did you reach the position you are currently in? Did you ever make a mistake in a job, how did you come back from it?

* * *

Development Topic:

What is one skill that you need to improve upon? Perhaps presenting, writing for publication, or managing people? How can you improve upon that skill? What are you three best skills? What skills would benefit you most in your current position?

* * *

Development Topic:

What is your desired career trajectory? Where do you see yourself in five year? What steps can you take now to get yourself closer to your goal? What holes, if any, are there in your resume? How do you ask my supervisor for a raise? How do you handle the stress of downsizing?

<u>9</u>

Welcome Email Example:

Congratulations! Welcome to the mentor program.

Get ready to have a year or fun, learning and growing. Your pair is: _____ and _____ both of you are included on this email.

Please mark your calendar for the initial introduction and retreat planned for <day/date/time> via zoom. A link will be emailed to you as the date gets closer.

Mark you calendar for the following dates as well:

- Initial Retreat
- Annual Conference (if you are going)

- Mid-way meeting
- Final Group Touch-Base

We are excited to have you on this journey and hope you are excited!

10

Retreat

EXAMPLE for Power Point slides:

1 - Introductions of your committee (5 minutes)

2- General ice-breaker for whole group (5-10 minutes)

3 - Break-out session for pairs or groups (2 minutes) learn all you can: hobbies, etc.

4 - Define mentoring, you can use a video or quotes, but get this down (5-7 minutes)

5 - Group discussion: think of a mentor YOU had, what did you like, not like, what

worked, or didn't work, what did you learn? (7-10 minutes)

6 - Benefits of being a Mentor / Mentee (10 minutes, 5 for mentor, 5 for mentee)

7 - BREAK (5 minutes)

8 - Mentors get together with each other in one room, and Menees get together in

their own room to idea share, talk about expectations. This is a great way for them

learn from each other. (10 minutes)

9 - Get back together to share out expectations from each

group (5-7 minutes)

10 - Talk about the expectation of the program, that you meet once a month at a

minimum, and explain how to goal setting works, see the SMART goal (Zachary &

Fischler, 2012) worksheet, or other. (5-7 minutes)

11 - Good place to put information about how to be a good mentor/mentee (5 minutes)

12 - Pairs now go into private rooms to set goals, and set up first meeting (10 minutes)

13 - End with a list of resources that you used in the presentation, as well as a list of

the upcoming dates and a reminder to commit to one meeting per month, at a

minimum (5-7 minutes)

About the Author

Jordan Wienke has experience in higher education, parks and recreation, presenting and writing. She has worked shaping mentoring programs in all her different professions. Today Wienke writes, learns and shares as often as she can.

Printed in Great Britain
by Amazon

42419387R00036